CLAUDE 3.5 EXPE

UNLOCK ADVANCED AI CAPABILITIES

HAWKINGS J CROWD

Preface

In the ever-accelerating realm of artificial intelligence, a new standard has emerged. Claude 3.5 represents a significant leap forward, pushing the boundaries of what's possible with natural language processing and multimodal AI. This book is your comprehensive guide to mastering this powerful technology, unlocking its advanced capabilities, and leveraging them to transform your work and creative endeavors.

Whether you're a seasoned developer, a curious researcher, or a business professional seeking to integrate cutting-edge AI into your workflows, this book is designed to provide you with the knowledge and skills necessary to harness the full potential of Claude 3.5. We'll delve into the core architecture that underpins its remarkable abilities, explore the nuances of prompt engineering, and demonstrate how to apply Claude 3.5 to a wide range of tasks, from content generation and data analysis to code development and ethical AI implementation.

This isn't just a theoretical exploration. We'll provide practical examples, actionable insights, and best practices gleaned from real-world applications. We'll explore the advancements that separate Claude 3.5 from its predecessors, and provide the tools to navigate the complexities of AI-driven communication.

As AI continues to reshape our world, understanding and effectively utilizing models like Claude 3.5 becomes increasingly crucial. This book aims to empower you to not only understand this technology but to become a proficient user, capable of creating innovative solutions and contributing to the responsible evolution of AI.

TABLE OF CONTENTS

Chapter 1

Introducing Claude 3.5: The Next Generation of AI

1.1 Understanding the Core Architecture of Claude 3.5"

To truly harness the power of Claude 3.5, we must first dissect its underlying architecture. This isn't just a matter of technical curiosity; it's about understanding the mechanisms that enable it to process and generate language with such remarkable fluency and nuance.

Claude 3.5, at its core, is a transformer-based language model. This architectural choice is pivotal, as it distinguishes it from earlier sequential models that processed language word by word. The transformer architecture allows Claude 3.5 to process entire sequences of words simultaneously, enabling it to capture complex relationships and dependencies within the text.

The Power of Attention:

The cornerstone of the transformer architecture is the "attention mechanism." This mechanism allows the model to weigh the importance of different words in a sequence, effectively focusing on the most relevant information. Imagine reading the sentence, "The cat chased the mouse, which ran quickly." The attention mechanism allows Claude 3.5 to recognize that "which" refers to "mouse," even though they are separated by other words.

This is achieved through "self-attention," where each word in the input sequence is compared to every other word. By assigning "attention scores" to these comparisons, the model can identify the relationships and dependencies between words, regardless of their position in the sequence. This is critical for understanding context and capturing the nuances of language.

Layered Processing:

Claude 3.5 utilizes a layered structure, where the input data is processed through multiple layers of self-attention and feed-forward neural networks. Each layer refines the model's understanding of the text, allowing it to progressively build a more comprehensive representation of the input.

Self-Attention Layers: These layers are responsible for identifying relationships between words within the input sequence.

Feed-Forward Neural Networks: These layers further process the output of the self-attention layers, refining the model's understanding of the text.

This layered structure allows Claude 3.5 to learn increasingly complex patterns in the data, enabling it to generate coherent and contextually relevant responses.

Contextual Understanding:

The architecture also plays a vital role in Claude 3.5's ability to maintain context. The model's context window, which determines the amount of text it can consider at any given time, is a critical factor in its performance. The transformer architecture makes it possible to efficiently manage this window.

In practical terms, this means that Claude 3.5 can maintain coherence over longer conversations and documents, allowing it to provide more relevant and informative responses.

By understanding these core architectural concepts, we can begin to appreciate the sophistication of Claude 3.5 and its ability to process and generate language with such remarkable proficiency.

1.2 Key Improvements and Features Over Previous Versions

Claude 3.5 represents a significant leap forward in AI capabilities, building upon the foundations laid by its predecessors. Understanding the specific enhancements and new features is essential to appreciate the advancements in this latest iteration.

Enhanced Context Window and Memory:

One of the most notable improvements in Claude 3.5 is the expansion of its context window. This allows the model to process and retain more information, leading to more coherent and contextually relevant responses. In practical terms, this means Claude 3.5 can handle longer documents, more complex conversations, and more intricate tasks without losing track of the context.

Increased Processing Capacity: This enables the model to effectively manage and utilize larger amounts of data.

Improved Long-Term Memory: This results in more consistent and accurate responses over extended interactions.

Advanced Reasoning and Problem-Solving:

Claude 3.5 demonstrates enhanced reasoning and problem-solving abilities. It can analyze complex information, identify patterns, and draw logical conclusions with greater accuracy. This improvement is particularly evident in tasks that require critical thinking, such as data analysis, research, and decision-making.

Enhanced Analytical Skills: The model can dissect complex problems and break them down into manageable components.

Improved Logical Inference: Claude 3.5 can draw more accurate and reliable conclusions from given information.

Refined Natural Language Understanding:

Claude 3.5 exhibits a deeper understanding of natural language, allowing it to interpret nuances, idioms, and subtle variations in meaning with greater precision. This improvement leads to more natural and intuitive interactions.

Improved Nuance Detection: The model can recognize and interpret subtle variations in language.

Enhanced Idiom Recognition: Claude 3.5 can accurately interpret idiomatic expressions and colloquialisms.

Multimodal Capabilities:

Claude 3.5 Sonnet has advanced vision capabilities. This is a large improvement over previous versions. The AI can now understand and process visual data, allowing for richer and more versatile interactions.

Image Analysis: Claude 3.5 can analyze images and extract relevant information.

Combined Text and Visual processing: The AI can understand and utilize both visual and textual information.

Enhanced Safety and Alignment:

Anthropic has continued to prioritize safety and alignment in Claude 3.5. The model has been further refined to adhere to ethical principles and avoid generating harmful or biased content.

This commitment to safety is evident in the model's responses, which are designed to be helpful, harmless, and honest.

Improved Constitutional AI: The model's adherence to ethical guidelines has been further strengthened.

Reduced Bias and Harmful Outputs: Claude 3.5 is designed to minimize the generation of biased or harmful content.

Improved Speed and Efficiency:

Claude 3.5 is designed to be faster and more efficient than previous versions. This improvement is essential for real-time applications, such as chatbots and virtual assistants, where users expect immediate responses.

Optimized Processing Pipelines: The model's architecture has been optimized for faster processing.

Reduced Latency: Claude 3.5 delivers faster and more responsive performance.

By highlighting these key improvements and features, we can appreciate the significant advancements in Claude 3.5 and its potential to revolutionize AI interactions.

1.3 Setting Up Your Development Environment

To effectively utilize Claude 3.5, a well-configured development environment is essential. This section will guide you through the necessary steps to set up your environment, ensuring a smooth and efficient workflow.

1. Accessing Claude 3.5:

API Access:

Claude 3.5 is primarily accessed through Anthropic's API. Therefore, you'll need to create an account on Anthropic's website and obtain API keys.

Explain the process of signing up, verifying your account, and navigating the Anthropic developer portal.

Detail how to generate and securely store your API keys, emphasizing the importance of keeping them confidential.

Choosing the Right Access Method:

Explain the different ways to interact with the API (e.g., using Python libraries, command-line tools, or web-based interfaces).

If possible explain the use of any specific IDE's that are most useful.

2. Programming Language and Libraries:

Python (Recommended):

Python is the most common language used to interact with AI APIs. Therefore, install the latest version of Python on your system.

Explain how to set up a virtual environment to isolate your project dependencies.

Detail the installation of the Anthropic Python client library using `pip`.

Other Languages (If Applicable):

If Anthropic provides SDKs or libraries for other languages (e.g., JavaScript, Node.js), provide instructions for setting them up.

Essential Libraries:

Besides the Anthropic client library, recommend other useful Python libraries, such as `requests` (for making HTTP requests), `json` (for handling JSON data), and `dotenv` (for managing environment variables).

3. Integrated Development Environment (IDE) or Text Editor:

Choosing an IDE:

Recommend popular IDEs like VS Code, PyCharm, or Jupyter Notebooks, explaining their advantages for AI development.

Provide tips for configuring the chosen IDE for Python development.

Text Editor Alternatives:

If readers prefer lightweight text editors, recommend options like Sublime Text or Atom, and explain how to configure them for Python.

4. Environment Variables:

Storing API Keys:

Explain the importance of storing API keys as environment variables rather than hardcoding them in your code.

Provide instructions for setting environment variables on different operating systems (Windows, macOS, Linux).

Show how to use the `dotenv` library to load environment variables from a `.env` file.

5. Testing the Setup:

Making a Simple API Call:

Provide a basic Python code snippet that makes a simple API call to Claude 3.5, such as generating a short text completion.

Explain how to run the code and verify that the API call is successful.

Explain how to read the returned JSON data.

Troubleshooting:

Provide common troubleshooting tips for issues that might arise during setup, such as API key errors, network connectivity problems, or library installation issues.

Chapter 2

Mastering Prompt Engineering for Optimal Results

2.1 Crafting Effective Prompts: Best Practices and Techniques"

The power of Claude 3.5 is unlocked through well-crafted prompts. A prompt is not just a question; it's a carefully constructed instruction that guides the AI to produce the desired output.[1] Mastering prompt engineering is crucial for maximizing the model's capabilities.[2]

Understanding the Anatomy of a Good Prompt:

Clarity and Specificity:

Avoid ambiguity.[3] Be precise about what you want Claude 3.5 to do.

Use concrete terms and provide context.

Example: Instead of "Summarize this," say "Summarize the key findings of this research paper, focusing on the implications for climate change."

Contextual Information:

Provide relevant background information to help Claude 3.5 understand the task.

Include any necessary constraints or limitations.

Example: "You are a historical expert. Given the following excerpt from a medieval text, explain the social structure of the time."

Desired Format:

Specify the format of the output you want.

This could be a paragraph, a list, a table, or a specific document structure.

Example: "Generate a list of five key points from this article, formatted as bullet points."

Tone and Style:

Indicate the desired tone and style of the response.

This could be formal, informal, technical, or creative.

Example: "Write a short story in a humorous tone, using the following characters."

Best Practices and Techniques:

Role-Playing:

Assign a specific role to Claude 3.5 to guide its responses.

Example: "You are a seasoned marketing consultant. Provide a strategy for launching this new product."

Few-Shot Prompting:

Provide a few examples of the desired output to guide the model.

This helps Claude 3.5 understand the pattern or style you're looking for.

Example: "Here are some examples of effective product descriptions: [Examples]. Now, write a product description for this item: [Item]."

Chain-of-Thought Prompting:

For complex tasks, prompt the model to break down the problem into smaller, logical steps.

This technique is especially useful for reasoning and problem-solving tasks.

Example: "First, identify the key variables in this equation. Then, explain how they relate to each other. Finally, solve the equation."

Iterative Refinement:

Don't be afraid to experiment with different prompts.

If the initial output is not satisfactory, refine your prompt and try again.

Example: If a summary is too short, request a more detailed summary.

Negative Constraints:

Tell the AI what not to do.

Example: "Do not include any personal opinions in your response."

Using Delimiters:

Using things like triple quotes, or triple dashes, can help the AI understand where sections of the prompt begin, and end.

Temperature Control:

Explain the concept of temperature within the API settings, and how it effects the randomness of the output.

2.2 Understanding Context and Nuance in AI Communication

Effective communication with AI, particularly models like Claude 3.5, goes beyond simply providing instructions. It requires a deep understanding of how context and nuance influence the AI's responses.

The Importance of Context:

Situational Context:

Claude 3.5 relies heavily on the context you provide. This includes the preceding conversation, the document you've uploaded, or any relevant background information.

Explain how changes in context can significantly alter the AI's responses.

Example: A question about "apples" will yield different answers depending on whether the context is a fruit basket or a technology company.

Temporal Context:

In conversational interactions, the AI maintains a memory of previous turns. This temporal context is crucial for maintaining coherence.

Explain how Claude 3.5 uses its context window to retain information from earlier parts of the conversation.

Explain how to reset the context when needed.

Domain-Specific Context:

Different fields have their own jargon, terminology, and conventions. Providing domain-specific context helps Claude 3.5 generate more accurate and relevant responses.

Example: A medical query requires a different context than a legal query.

Navigating Nuance:

Subtleties of Language:

Nuance refers to the subtle variations in meaning that can arise from word choice, tone, and phrasing.

Explain how Claude 3.5 is designed to recognize and interpret these subtleties.

Example: The difference between "suggest" and "demand."

Idioms and Figurative Language:

Idioms, metaphors, and other forms of figurative language can be challenging for AI.

Explain how Claude 3.5 handles these linguistic complexities.

Explain how to help the AI understand these complex uses of language.

Emotional Tone:

AI models are increasingly capable of understanding and responding to emotional tone.

Explain how Claude 3.5 can detect and adapt to different emotional cues.

Explain the limitations of the AI regarding emotional understanding.

Cultural Nuances:

Different cultures have different ways of expressing themselves. Explain how cultural differences can effect the AI's output.

Explain how to provide cultural context to the AI.

Implicit vs. Explicit Communication:

Humans often communicate implicitly, relying on shared knowledge and assumptions.

Explain the importance of being explicit when communicating with AI, to avoid misunderstandings.

Techniques for Enhancing Context and Nuance:

Providing Detailed Background Information:

The more context you provide, the better Claude 3.5 can understand your request.

Using Clear and Unambiguous Language:

Avoid jargon or overly complex phrasing, unless it is needed for the specific context.

Testing and Iterating:

Experiment with different prompts and observe how Claude 3.5 responds to subtle changes in wording.

Few shot prompting:

Providing a few examples can help the AI understand the desired context, and nuance.

By understanding the importance of context and nuance, you can significantly improve the quality of your interactions with Claude 3.5.

2.3 Advanced Prompting Strategies for Specific Tasks

While basic prompting can yield useful results, advanced prompting techniques are essential for tackling complex tasks and maximizing the potential of Claude 3.5. These strategies are tailored to specific types of tasks, enabling you to achieve more precise and nuanced outputs.

1. Task Decomposition and Chain-of-Thought:

Complex Problem Solving:

For tasks requiring multi-step reasoning, decompose the problem into smaller, manageable sub-tasks.

Use "chain-of-thought" prompting to guide Claude 3.5 through each step, encouraging it to explain its reasoning.

Example: "To solve this complex mathematical equation, first, identify the variables. Then, explain the relationships between them. Next, apply the relevant formulas. Finally, provide the solution."

Logical Reasoning:

Prompt the model to follow a logical sequence of steps, explicitly stating the premises and conclusions.

This helps the model avoid logical fallacies and generate more reliable outputs.

2. Role-Playing and Persona Assignment:

Expert Simulation:

Assign a specific persona or role to Claude 3.5 to guide its responses.

This technique is particularly useful for tasks requiring specialized knowledge or expertise.

Example: "You are a seasoned legal expert. Analyze this contract and provide a summary of the key clauses and potential legal risks."

Audience Targeting:

Instruct the model to tailor its responses to a specific audience, considering their background, knowledge level, and interests.

Example: "Explain the concept of quantum computing to a high school student, using simple language and relatable examples."

3. Iterative Refinement and Feedback Loops:

Prompt Engineering as a Process:

View prompt engineering as an iterative process, where you refine your prompts based on the model's outputs.

Use feedback loops to identify areas for improvement and adjust your prompts accordingly.

Example: If the model's initial response is too general, provide more specific instructions and ask it to elaborate on certain points.

Using Constraints and Boundaries:

Adding constraints to the prompt can greatly refine the output.

Example: "Write a poem that is exactly 14 lines long, and uses a ABAB rhyme scheme."

4. Data Extraction and Structured Output:

Information Retrieval:

Prompt the model to extract specific information from unstructured text, such as documents or web pages.

Specify the format of the desired output, such as a table, list, or JSON object.

Example: "From the following article, extract the names of all the companies mentioned, and their stock ticker symbols, and return the data as a JSON object."

Generating Structured Content:

Instruct the model to generate structured content, such as code, tables, or data schemas.

Provide clear instructions on the desired format and structure.

5. Few-Shot Learning and Pattern Recognition:

Demonstrating Desired Output:

Provide a few examples of the desired output to guide the model's responses.

This technique is particularly useful for tasks involving pattern recognition or style imitation.

Example: "Here are a few examples of how to write a good tweet: [examples]. Now write a tweet about this topic: [topic]"

Adapting to Specific Styles:

Few shot learning can be used to make the AI mimic a specific writing style.

By mastering these advanced prompting strategies, you can unlock the full potential of Claude 3.5 and achieve remarkable results in a wide range of tasks.

Chapter 3

Leveraging Claude 3.5 for Content Creation and Generation

3.1 Generating High-Quality Text: Articles, Reports, and Creative Writing

Claude 3.5 excels at generating high-quality text, making it a powerful tool for various writing tasks, including articles, reports, and creative writing.[1] Understanding how to effectively prompt the model is crucial for achieving the desired results.

1. Articles and Informative Content:

Research and Summarization:

Prompt Claude 3.5 to research a topic and summarize key findings from multiple sources.

Specify the desired length, tone, and target audience for the article.

Example: "Research the latest advancements in renewable energy and write a 1,000-word article for a general audience, focusing on the benefits of solar and wind power."

Structured Content Creation:

Instruct the model to generate articles with a clear structure, including headings, subheadings, and bullet points.

Provide an outline or a list of key points to guide the model.

Example: "Write an article about the history of the internet. Use the following structure: Introduction, Early Development, The World Wide Web, Social Media, Future Trends."

Fact-Checking and Verification:

Prompt the model to verify information and provide citations for its sources.

This helps ensure the accuracy and reliability of the generated content.

Example: "Write an article about the impact of climate change on coastal cities. Please include factual data, and where you got that data from."

2. Reports and Technical Writing:

Data Analysis and Interpretation:

Prompt Claude 3.5 to analyze data and generate reports with clear visualizations and explanations.

Specify the desired format for the report, such as a PDF or Word document.

Example: "Analyze this sales data and generate a report summarizing the key trends and insights, including charts and graphs."

Technical Documentation:

Instruct the model to generate technical documentation, such as user manuals, API documentation, or code comments.

Provide clear instructions on the desired level of detail and technical accuracy.

Example: "Generate API documentation for this Python function, including input parameters, output values, and error handling."

Summarizing Long Documents:

Claude 3.5 can condense large reports into smaller more manageable summaries.

Example: "Please provide a one page summary of this 100 page legal document."

3. Creative Writing:

Story Generation:

Prompt Claude 3.5 to generate stories with compelling characters, plot twists, and vivid descriptions.

Provide a starting point, such as a character, setting, or theme.

Example: "Write a short story about a detective who investigates a mysterious disappearance in a small town."

Poetry and Songwriting:

Instruct the model to generate poems or song lyrics with specific rhyme schemes, meter, or themes.[2]

Provide examples of the desired style or genre.

Example: "Write a sonnet about the beauty of nature, using iambic pentameter."

Scriptwriting:

Claude 3.5 can be used to generate scripts for plays, movies, or TV shows.

Example: "Write a script for a short comedy skit about two friends who get lost in the woods."

Adapting to specific writing styles:

Using few shot learning, you can have the AI mimic the writing style of famous authors.

Key Considerations:

Prompt Clarity:

Clearly define your requirements and provide sufficient context.

Iterative Refinement:

Refine your prompts based on the model's outputs to achieve the desired results.

Ethical Considerations:

Be mindful of potential biases or harmful content in the generated text.

Always fact check the AI's output.

3.2 Content Summarization and Information Extraction Techniques

Claude 3.5's ability to condense large volumes of text and extract specific data points makes it a valuable tool for information management. This section explores various techniques for content summarization and information extraction.

1. Content Summarization Techniques:

Extractive Summarization:

This technique involves selecting key sentences or phrases from the original text and combining them to form a summary.

Claude 3.5 can identify the most important sentences based on their relevance and frequency.

Example: "Extract the most important sentences from this article to create a concise summary."

Abstractive Summarization:

This technique involves generating a summary that captures the main ideas of the original text, even if it uses different words and phrases.

Claude 3.5 can understand the context and meaning of the text, allowing it to create accurate and coherent summaries.

Example: "Summarize this research paper in your own words, focusing on the key findings and implications."

Query-Based Summarization:

This technique involves generating a summary that focuses on specific aspects of the original text, based on a user's query.

Claude 3.5 can identify and extract relevant information related to the query.

Example: "Summarize this news article, focusing on the financial impact of the event."

Summarization with Length Constraints:

Adding constraints to the prompt, such as word count, or sentence count, can greatly refine the summarization.

Example: "Summarize this document in 3 sentences."

2. Information Extraction Techniques:

Named Entity Recognition (NER):

This technique involves identifying and extracting named entities, such as people, organizations, locations, and dates, from the text

Claude 3.5 can identify and classify these entities with high accuracy.

Example: "Extract all the names of people and organizations mentioned in this article."

Relationship Extraction:

This technique involves identifying and extracting relationships between entities, such as "works for," "located in," or "is a part of."

Claude 3.5 can identify and extract these relationships based on the context of the text.

Example: "Extract the relationships between the companies and their products mentioned in this document."

Keyword Extraction:

This technique involves identifying and extracting the most important keywords or phrases from the text.

Claude 3.5 can identify and extract these keywords based on their frequency and relevance.

Example: "Extract the key keywords from this research paper."

Data Extraction into Structured Formats:

Claude 3.5 can be prompted to extract information, and then place that information into a structured format such as JSON, or CSV.

This is very useful for taking unstructured data, and placing it into a database.

Example: "Extract all of the addresses, and phone numbers from this document, and return the data as a JSON object."

Sentiment analysis:

Claude 3.5 can analyze text, and determine the sentiment of the text.

Example: "Analyze the following customer reviews, and determine if the overall sentiment is positive, negative, or neutral."

3. Techniques for Enhancing Accuracy:

Providing Context:

The more context you provide, the more accurate the results will be.

Using Clear and Specific Prompts:

Avoid ambiguity and clearly define your requirements.

Iterative Refinement:

Refine your prompts based on the model's outputs to achieve the desired results.

Few shot learning:

Providing a few examples of the desired output can greatly increase the accuracy of the extraction.

By mastering these techniques, you can effectively leverage Claude 3.5 to summarize large volumes of text and extract valuable information.

3.3 Adapting Claude 3.5 for Different Writing Styles and Tones

Claude 3.5's versatility extends to its ability to adapt to a wide range of writing styles and tones. This makes it a valuable tool for creating content that resonates with specific audiences and purposes.

1. Understanding Writing Styles:

Formal vs. Informal

Explain the differences between formal and informal writing styles, including vocabulary, sentence structure, and tone.

Provide examples of prompts that elicit formal and informal writing.

Example (Formal): "Write a report summarizing the findings of this research paper, using formal language and academic tone."

Example (Informal): "Write a blog post about your favorite hobby, using casual language and a friendly tone."

Technical vs. Conversational:

Explain the differences between technical and conversational writing styles, including the level of jargon, complexity, and formality.

Provide examples of prompts that elicit technical and conversational writing.

Example (Technical): "Write a technical manual explaining how to configure a network router, using precise terminology and detailed instructions."

Example (Conversational): "Write a blog post explaining a complex scientific concept in simple, easy-to-understand language."

Creative vs. Analytical:

Explain the differences between creative and analytical writing styles, including the use of imagery, storytelling, and logical reasoning.

Provide examples of prompts that elicit creative and analytical writing.

Example (Creative): "Write a short story about a magical adventure, using vivid descriptions and imaginative language."

Example (Analytical): "Write an essay analyzing the economic impact of a recent policy change, using data and logical arguments."

Mimicking Specific Authors:

Few shot learning can be used to have the AI mimic the writing style of specific authors.

Example: "Here are a few examples of Ernest Hemingway's writing style: [examples]. Now write a short story in the style of Ernest Hemingway."

2. Understanding Tones

Positive vs. Negative:

Explain how to prompt Claude 3.5 to adopt a positive or negative tone, depending on the context.

Example (Positive): "Write a customer review praising the excellent service and high-quality product."

Example (Negative): "Write a customer review expressing disappointment with the poor service and defective product."

Humorous vs. Serious:

Explain how to prompt Claude 3.5 to adopt a humorous or serious tone, depending on the desired effect.

Example (Humorous): "Write a funny story about a clumsy waiter who spills food on customers."

Example (Serious): "Write a news report about a tragic accident, using a somber and respectful tone."

Persuasive vs. Informative:

Explain how to prompt Claude 3.5 to adopt a persuasive or informative tone, depending on the purpose of the content.

Example (Persuasive): "Write a persuasive essay arguing for the benefits of renewable energy."

Example (Informative): "Write a report summarizing the key findings of a scientific study."

Emotional tones:

Claude 3.5 can be prompted to write with various emotional tones, such as excited, sad, angry, or happy.

3. Techniques for Adapting Style and Tone:

Providing Explicit Instructions:

Clearly state the desired writing style and tone in your prompt.

Using Example Prompts:

Provide examples of text that exhibit the desired style and tone.

Iterative Refinement:

Refine your prompts based on the model's outputs to achieve the desired results.

Using Role Playing:

Assigning a role to the AI can greatly influence the tone, and style of the output.

By mastering these techniques, you can effectively adapt Claude 3.5 to generate content that aligns with your specific needs and preferences.

Chapter 4

Data Analysis and Interpretation with Claude 3.5

4.1 Processing and Analyzing Large Datasets Using Natural Language"

Claude 3.5's ability to understand and generate natural language opens up new possibilities for interacting with and analyzing large datasets. Instead of relying solely on traditional programming languages and statistical tools, users can leverage natural language to query, explore, and derive insights from data.

1. Data Loading and Preparation:

Natural Language Data Ingestion:

Explain how Claude 3.5 can process data from various sources, including CSV files, JSON files, text documents, and even web pages, using natural language descriptions.

Example: "Load the data from 'sales_data.csv' and describe the columns."

Data Cleaning and Preprocessing:

Demonstrate how to use natural language to instruct Claude 3.5 to clean and preprocess data, such as handling missing values, standardizing formats, and removing duplicates.

Example: "Remove any rows with missing values in the 'price' column and convert the 'date' column to a consistent format."

Data Transformation:

Show how to use natural language to transform data, such as creating new columns, aggregating data, and filtering rows.

Example: "Create a new column called 'total_revenue' by multiplying the 'quantity' and 'price' columns. Then, filter the data to include only sales from the 'electronics' category."

2. Data Exploration and Analysis:

Natural Language Queries:

Explain how to use natural language to ask questions about the data and retrieve specific information.

Example: "What is the average sales revenue for each product category?"

Show how to ask more complex questions that involve multiple conditions and calculations.

Descriptive Statistics:

Demonstrate how to use natural language to generate descriptive statistics, such as mean, median, standard deviation, and percentiles.

Example: "Calculate the mean and standard deviation of the 'age' column."

Trend Analysis:

Show how to use natural language to identify trends and patterns in the data, such as seasonal variations, correlations, and outliers.

Example: "Identify any seasonal trends in the sales data."

Data Visualization:

Explain how Claude 3.5 can help generate descriptions of charts and graphs.

Example: "Describe what this bar chart is showing me."

Generating hypotheses:

Claude 3.5 can be prompted to generate possible hypotheses from the data, which can then be tested.

Example: "Based on this data, what are some possible reasons for the increase in sales during the summer months?"

3. Techniques for Enhancing Accuracy and Efficiency:

Providing Context and Constraints:

Clearly define the data source, the columns of interest, and any relevant constraints.

Example: "Using the 'customer_data.csv' file, find the number of customers in each city, but only include cities with more than 100 customers."

Iterative Refinement:

Start with simple queries and gradually refine them based on the model's responses.

Use feedback loops to correct errors and improve the accuracy of the analysis.

Using Examples:

Providing a few examples of the desired output can greatly enhance the models performance.

Combining Natural Language with Code:

Explain how Claude 3.5 can assist in generating code snippets (e.g., Python code) to perform more complex data analysis tasks.

This allows users to seamlessly transition between natural language and code-based analysis.

By leveraging natural language, users can make data analysis more accessible and intuitive, enabling them to derive valuable insights from large datasets without requiring extensive programming or statistical expertise.

4.2 Extracting Insights and Patterns from Unstructured Data"

Unstructured data, such as text documents, social media posts, and customer reviews, contains a wealth of valuable information. Claude 3.5's natural language processing capabilities make it a powerful tool for extracting insights and patterns from this type of data.

1. Text Analysis and Topic Modeling:

Topic Extraction:

Explain how Claude 3.5 can identify and extract key topics from large collections of text documents.

Demonstrate how to use natural language to prompt the model to generate topic summaries and keywords.

Example: "Analyze these customer reviews and identify the main topics discussed."

Sentiment Analysis:

Show how to use natural language to determine the sentiment (positive, negative, or neutral) expressed in text data.

Explain how to prompt the model to identify and extract specific sentiment-related phrases or keywords.

Example: "Analyze these social media posts and determine the overall sentiment towards the new product launch."

Trend Detection:

Demonstrate how to use natural language to identify emerging trends and patterns in text data over time.

Example: "Analyze these news articles and identify any emerging trends in the technology industry."

2. Information Extraction and Knowledge Discovery:

Named Entity Recognition (NER):

Explain how Claude 3.5 can identify and extract named entities, such as people, organizations, and locations, from unstructured text.

Example: "Extract all the names of companies and their CEOs mentioned in these news articles."

Relationship Extraction:

Show how to use natural language to identify and extract relationships between entities, such as "works for," "located in," or "is a part of."

Example: "Extract the relationships between the companies and their products mentioned in these customer reviews."

Knowledge Graph Construction:

Explain how to use Claude 3.5 to extract entities and relationships from unstructured data and construct knowledge graphs.

This allows for the visualization and exploration of complex relationships between entities.

Example: "Extract the entities and relationships from these research papers and construct a knowledge graph."

3. Techniques for Enhancing Accuracy and Efficiency:

Providing Context and Constraints:

Clearly define the data source, the type of information you want to extract, and any relevant constraints.

Example: "From these customer reviews, extract all the complaints about the product's durability, but only include reviews from the past month."

Using Clear and Specific Prompts:

Avoid ambiguity and clearly define your requirements.

Iterative Refinement:

Start with simple queries and gradually refine them based on the model's responses.

Use feedback loops to correct errors and improve the accuracy of the analysis.

Few shot learning:

Providing examples of the desired output can greatly increase the accuracy of the extraction.

Combining with Structured Data:

If possible, combine extracted unstructured data with structured data to gain even more insights.

Example: combining customer review sentiment, with customer purchasing history.

By leveraging natural language processing, users can effectively extract valuable insights and patterns from unstructured data, enabling them to make informed decisions and gain a deeper understanding of complex phenomena.

4.3 Using Claude 3.5 to Generate Data Reports and Visualizations"

Claude 3.5 can significantly streamline the process of creating data reports and visualizations. While it doesn't directly generate visual charts itself, it excels at interpreting data, describing visualizations, and generating the textual components of reports.

1. Generating Textual Components of Data Reports:

Executive Summaries:

Explain how Claude 3.5 can analyze data and generate concise executive summaries that highlight key findings and insights.

Example: "Analyze this sales data and generate a one-paragraph executive summary highlighting the key trends and performance metrics."

Data Interpretations:

Show how to use natural language to prompt Claude 3.5 to interpret data and explain its significance.

Example: "Explain the meaning of the correlation coefficient between these two variables."

Methodology Descriptions:

Demonstrate how to generate clear and concise descriptions of the data analysis methodology used in a report.

Example: "Describe the steps taken to clean and preprocess this dataset."

Generating report outlines:

Claude 3.5 can be used to generate report outlines, which can then be used to create the full report.

Example: "Generate an outline for a report on the impact of social media on mental health."

Generating conclusions and recommendations:

Claude 3.5 can analyze data and generate conclusions and recommendations based on the findings.

Example: "Based on this customer feedback data, generate three recommendations for improving customer satisfaction."

2. Describing and Interpreting Visualizations:

Chart and Graph Descriptions:

Explain how Claude 3.5 can analyze and describe the key features and trends depicted in charts and graphs.

Example: "Describe the trends shown in this line graph of website traffic over time."

Data Visualization Explanations:

Show how to use natural language to prompt Claude 3.5 to explain the meaning and implications of data visualizations.

Example: "Explain what this pie chart is telling me about the distribution of customer demographics."

Identifying Anomalies and Outliers:

Claude 3.5 can assist in identifying anomalies and outliers in visualizations and explain their potential significance.

Example: "Describe any unusual patterns or outliers in this scatter plot and explain their possible causes."

Generating figure captions:

Claude 3.5 can be used to generate informative and concise figure captions for charts and graphs.

Example: "Generate a caption for this bar chart showing the sales revenue for each product category."

3. Enhancing Report Generation Workflow:

Data Storytelling:

Explain how Claude 3.5 can help craft compelling data narratives by weaving together data insights and contextual information.

Example: "Tell a story about the impact of this marketing campaign using the provided sales data."

Automating Report Generation:

Demonstrate how to integrate Claude 3.5 with data analysis tools and reporting platforms to automate the generation of data reports.

This will likely involve generating code, or structured data, that other programs can then use.

Improving accessibility:

Claude 3.5 can be used to generate alt text for images, and descriptions of charts, which can improve the accessibility of reports.

Example: "Generate alt text for this image of a bar chart."

Key Considerations:

Accuracy and Reliability:

While Claude 3.5 can assist in generating data reports and visualizations, it's essential to verify the accuracy of the generated content.

Data Privacy:

Be mindful of data privacy considerations when using Claude 3.5 to analyze and generate reports from sensitive data.

Tool Integration:

Claude 3.5 is a language model, so to produce actual charts and graphs, the user will need to use other programs. Claude 3.5 can produce the text that goes along with those charts.

By leveraging Claude 3.5, users can enhance their data reporting and visualization workflows, making them more efficient and insightful.

Chapter 5

Implementing Claude 3.5 in Software Development

5.1 Integrating Claude 3.5 with Existing Applications and Systems"

Integrating Claude 3.5 with existing applications and systems opens up a world of possibilities for enhancing functionality and user experience. Here's a breakdown of how this integration can be achieved:

1. API-Based Integration:

RESTful API:

Claude 3.5 is primarily accessed through its API, which allows developers to send requests and receive responses in a standardized format (JSON).

This enables seamless integration with web applications, mobile apps, and other systems that support HTTP requests.

Authentication and Authorization:

Securely manage API keys and authentication tokens to control access to Claude 3.5's capabilities.

Implement authorization mechanisms to ensure that only authorized users or systems can interact with the API.

Data Exchange:

Format data in a way that Claude 3.5 can understand, such as JSON or plain text.

Process the API's JSON responses to extract the desired information and integrate it into your application.

2. Use Cases and Implementation:

Chatbots and Virtual Assistants:

Embed Claude 3.5 into chatbots to provide natural language conversations and personalized assistance.

Integrate with messaging platforms or custom interfaces to create seamless user experiences.

Content Generation and Automation:

Use Claude 3.5 to automate content creation tasks, such as generating product descriptions, writing reports, or summarizing documents.

Integrate with content management systems or workflow automation tools.

Data Analysis and Reporting:

Leverage Claude 3.5 to analyze data, extract insights, and generate reports in natural language.

Integrate with data visualization tools or business intelligence platforms.

Customer Service and Support:

Enhance customer service by using Claude 3.5 to answer frequently asked questions, resolve issues, and provide personalized support.

Integrate with CRM systems or help desk software.

Search and Information Retrieval:

Improve search functionality by using Claude 3.5 to understand natural language queries and retrieve relevant information from databases or knowledge bases.

Integrate with search engines or enterprise search platforms.

Code integration:

As shown in the example code, Claude 3.5 can be integrated with python, and other programming languages. The API can be used to add the AI's functionality to pre-existing code.

3. Considerations for Integration:

API Rate Limits:

Be aware of API rate limits and implement strategies to avoid exceeding them, such as caching responses or implementing queuing mechanisms.

Error Handling:

Implement robust error handling to gracefully handle API errors and unexpected responses.

Data Security and Privacy:

Ensure that sensitive data is protected during transmission and storage, and comply with relevant data privacy regulations.

Scalability and Performance:

Design your integration to handle increasing workloads and maintain optimal performance.

Latency:

Be mindful of the latency inherent in API calls, and design your application to handle potential delays.

5.2 Building AI-Powered Chatbots and Virtual Assistants"

Building AI-powered chatbots and virtual assistants with Claude 3.5 involves combining the model's natural language understanding and generation capabilities with a framework for handling conversations and user interactions. Here's a detailed guide:

1. Defining the Chatbot's Purpose and Scope:

Identify the Use Case:

Determine the specific tasks the chatbot will perform (e.g., customer support, information retrieval, task automation).

Clearly define the chatbot's domain and limitations.

Define Target Audience:

Consider the characteristics of the users who will interact with the chatbot.

Tailor the chatbot's language and tone to match the target audience.

Establish Key Features:

List the essential functionalities the chatbot must provide.

Prioritize features based on user needs and business goals.

2. Designing the Conversation Flow:

Create a Dialogue Script:

Map out potential user interactions and the chatbot's corresponding responses.

Consider different user intents and possible conversation paths.

Implement Intent Recognition:

Use Claude 3.5 to analyze user input and identify their intent.

Design a system to map user intents to specific chatbot actions.

Handle Context and Memory:

Implement a mechanism to maintain conversation context and user history.

Use Claude 3.5's context window to remember previous interactions.

Design Error Handling:

Create fallback responses for unexpected user input or errors.

Provide clear and helpful error messages.

3. Integrating Claude 3.5:

API Integration:

Use Claude 3.5's API to send user input and receive chatbot responses.

Implement API calls within your chatbot's framework.

Prompt Engineering:

Craft effective prompts to guide Claude 3.5's responses.

Use role-playing, few-shot learning, and other techniques to improve accuracy.

Data Processing:

Process user input and Claude 3.5's output to extract relevant information.

Format data for seamless integration with other systems.

4. Building the Chatbot Framework:

Choose a Platform:

Select a suitable platform or framework for building your chatbot (e.g., Python libraries, cloud-based chatbot platforms).

Python libraries like Flask or Django are very useful.

Implement User Interface:

Design a user-friendly interface for interacting with the chatbot.

Consider different channels, such as web chat, messaging apps, or voice assistants.

Develop Core Logic:

Implement the chatbot's core logic, including intent recognition, dialogue management, and data processing.

Consider using state machines to control the flow of the conversation.

5. Testing and Deployment:

Thorough Testing:

Conduct extensive testing to ensure the chatbot's accuracy, reliability, and user-friendliness.

Test different conversation scenarios and edge cases.

Deployment:

Deploy the chatbot to a suitable hosting environment.

Monitor performance and make necessary adjustments.

Continuous Improvement:

Collect user feedback and analyze chatbot performance to identify areas for improvement.

Regularly update the chatbot's knowledge base and dialogue scripts.

Example Code Snippet (Python):

```python
Python
import anthropic

client = anthropic.Client("YOUR_API_KEY")

def get_chatbot_response(user_input, conversation_history=""):
```

```python
        prompt = f"{conversation_history}\n\nUser: {user_input}\n\nAssistant:"
    response = client.completions.create(
        model="claude-3.5-sonnet",
        max_tokens_to_sample=200,
        prompt=prompt,
    )
    return response.completion

conversation = ""
while True:
    user_input = input("You: ")
    response = get_chatbot_response(user_input, conversation)
    print("Chatbot:", response)
        conversation += f"\n\nUser: {user_input}\n\nAssistant: {response}"
```

By following these steps, you can create powerful and engaging AI-powered chatbots and virtual assistants that enhance user experiences and automate tasks.

5.3 Utilizing Claude 3.5 for Code Generation and Debugging"

Utilizing Claude 3.5 for code generation and debugging can significantly streamline the software development process. Here's a detailed explanation of how to leverage its capabilities:

1. Code Generation:

Generating Code Snippets:

Claude 3.5 can generate code snippets in various programming languages based on natural language descriptions.

Example: "Generate a Python function that calculates the factorial of a given number."

Provide clear and specific instructions regarding the desired functionality, input parameters, and output values.

Creating Function and Class Definitions:

Instruct Claude 3.5 to generate function or class definitions, including method signatures and basic implementations.

Example: "Create a Java class called 'BankAccount' with methods for depositing and withdrawing funds."

Generating Boilerplate Code:

Use Claude 3.5 to generate boilerplate code for common tasks, such as setting up web servers, creating database connections, or implementing API endpoints

This can save developers time and effort by automating repetitive tasks.

Generating Documentation:

Claude 3.5 can be used to generate code comments, and documentation.

Example: "Generate comments for this python function, explaining what it does, and what the input parameters are."

Generating test cases:

Claude 3.5 can generate basic test cases for code.

Example: "Generate a few test cases for this function."

2. Debugging:

Identifying Code Errors:

Provide Claude 3.5 with code snippets and error messages, and ask it to identify potential errors.

Example: "This Python code throws a 'TypeError' when I run it. Can you identify the error?"

Explaining Code Behavior:

Use Claude 3.5 to explain the behavior of code snippets, helping developers understand how the code works.

Example: "Explain what this JavaScript function does and how it manipulates the DOM."

Suggesting Code Fixes:

Instruct Claude 3.5 to suggest code fixes for identified errors or bugs.

Example: "How can I fix this 'IndexError' in my Python code?"

Code Refactoring:

Claude 3.5 can suggest ways to refactor code to improve its readability, efficiency, or maintainability.

Example: "How can I refactor this code to make it more efficient?"

Understanding Error Messages:

Claude 3.5 can be used to explain complex error messages.

Example: "Explain what this long C++ compiler error message means."

3. Best Practices:

Provide Clear and Specific Instructions:

The more detailed your instructions, the better Claude 3.5 can understand your requirements.

Use Code Examples:

Provide code examples to illustrate the desired functionality or coding style.

Iterative Refinement:

Start with simple prompts and gradually refine them based on the model's responses.

Verify Code Output:

Always verify the generated code and test it thoroughly.

Combine with Human Expertise:

Use Claude 3.5 as a tool to assist with code generation and debugging, but always rely on human expertise for critical tasks.

Security Concerns:

Be aware of security risks when using AI to generate code. Always review generated code for potential vulnerabilities.

Few shot learning:

Providing a few examples of code, can help the AI understand the desired coding style.

By utilizing Claude 3.5 effectively, developers can enhance their productivity and improve the quality of their code.

Chapter 6

Enhancing Productivity and Workflow Automation

6.1 Automating Repetitive Tasks with Claude 3.5"

Automating repetitive tasks with Claude 3.5 can significantly boost productivity and efficiency. By leveraging its natural language processing and code generation capabilities, you can streamline workflows and free up valuable time. Here's how:

1. Identifying Repetitive Tasks:

Data Entry and Extraction:

Tasks like transferring data between spreadsheets, databases, or documents.

Extracting specific information from emails, PDFs, or web pages.

Content Creation and Summarization:

Generating product descriptions, social media posts, or reports.

Summarizing lengthy documents or articles.

Customer Service and Support:

Answering frequently asked questions or resolving common customer issues

Generating automated responses to emails or chat messages.

Code Generation and Debugging:

Generating boilerplate code, creating test cases, or debugging simple errors.

Generating documentation.

Data Analysis and Reporting:

Generating basic data reports.

Generating summaries of data.

Scheduling and Reminders:

Setting up reminders based on natural language inputs.

Generating scheduled reports.

2. Designing Automation Workflows:

Define Task Inputs and Outputs:

Clearly identify the data or information required to perform the task and the desired output format.

Break Down Tasks into Smaller Steps:

Divide complex tasks into simpler, manageable steps that can be automated using Claude 3.5.

Use Natural Language Prompts:

Craft clear and specific prompts that instruct Claude 3.5 to perform each step of the task.

Integrate with Existing Tools and Systems:

Use Claude 3.5's API to connect with other applications, databases, or cloud services.

Use python, or other programming languages, to make the connections.

Implement Error Handling:

Design workflows to handle potential errors or unexpected inputs.

Use code to handle errors.

3. Implementing Automation with Claude 3.5:

API Calls and Data Processing:

Use Claude 3.5's API to send prompts and receive responses.

Process the API's JSON responses to extract the desired information.

Code Generation for Automation Scripts:

Use Claude 3.5 to generate code snippets or scripts that automate specific tasks.

Example: "Generate a Python script that extracts email addresses from a text file."

Workflow Orchestration:

Combine multiple Claude 3.5 prompts and code snippets to create complex automation workflows.

Use programming languages or workflow automation tools to orchestrate the process.

Scheduled Automation:

Use task schedulers or cloud-based automation platforms to run automated tasks at specific intervals.

Example: using cron jobs to run python scripts.

4. Examples of Automation:

Automated Email Summarization:

Use Claude 3.5 to summarize incoming emails and extract key information.

Create a script that sends a daily summary of important emails to a specific channel.

Automated Data Entry:

Use Claude 3.5 to extract data from PDFs or scanned documents and automatically enter it into a database.

Automated Social Media Content Generation:

Use Claude 3.5 to generate social media posts based on product descriptions or news articles.

Example: "Generate 5 tweets based on the following news article: [article text]"

Automated Report Generation:

Use Claude 3.5 to summarize data, and write reports.

Example: "Generate a weekly sales report, based on the data in this CSV file."

5. Key Considerations:

Security:

Protect sensitive data and API keys when automating tasks.

Accuracy:

Verify the accuracy of Claude 3.5's outputs, especially for critical tasks.

Maintainability:

Design automation workflows that are easy to maintain and update.

Testing:

Thoroughly test all automation workflows.

By automating repetitive tasks with Claude 3.5, you can free up valuable time and resources, allowing you to focus on more strategic and creative work.

6.2 Creating Custom AI Workflows for Specific Industries"

Creating custom AI workflows for specific industries with Claude 3.5 involves tailoring the model's capabilities to address the unique challenges and requirements of each sector. Here's a breakdown of how to approach this:

1. Industry-Specific Needs Assessment:

Identify Pain Points:

Conduct thorough research to understand the specific challenges and inefficiencies within the target industry.

Interview industry experts and stakeholders to gather insights into their workflows.

Analyze Data and Processes:

Examine the types of data used in the industry and the processes involved in handling that data.

Identify opportunities for automation and optimization.

Define Key Objectives:

Clearly define the goals of the AI workflow, such as improving efficiency, reducing costs, or enhancing customer experience.

Establish measurable metrics to track the success of the workflow.

2. Customizing Claude 3.5 for Industry-Specific Tasks:

Prompt Engineering for Domain-Specific Language:

Train Claude 3.5 to understand and generate language specific to the industry's terminology and jargon.

Use few-shot learning with industry-specific examples to improve accuracy.

Data Integration with Industry-Specific Databases:

Develop API integrations to connect Claude 3.5 with industry-specific databases and data sources.

Enable the model to access and process relevant data in real time.

Workflow Automation for Industry-Specific Processes:

Design custom workflows that automate key processes within the industry, such as document processing, data analysis, or customer support.

Use code, and other tools, to connect Claude 3.5 to other systems.

Creating Industry-Specific Knowledge Bases:

Build knowledge bases containing industry-specific information, such as regulations, best practices, or product catalogs.

Use Claude 3.5 to access and retrieve information from these knowledge bases.

3. Examples of Industry-Specific AI Workflows:

Healthcare:

Automate medical record summarization and analysis.

Develop AI-powered chatbots for patient support and appointment scheduling.

Use Claude 3.5 to analyze medical research papers and identify relevant findings.

Finance:

Automate fraud detection and risk assessment.

Generate personalized financial reports and recommendations.

Develop AI-powered chatbots for customer service and financial advice.

Legal:

Automate legal document review and analysis.

Generate legal briefs and contracts.

Develop AI-powered chatbots for legal information retrieval.

Retail:

Automate product description generation and inventory management.

Develop AI-powered chatbots for customer service and personalized recommendations.

Use Claude 3.5 to analyze customer reviews and identify product trends.

Manufacturing:

Automate quality control and predictive maintenance.

Generate production reports and optimize supply chain management.

Develop AI-powered chatbots for equipment troubleshooting.

Education:

Automate the generation of personalized learning materials.

Develop AI-powered tutoring systems.

Use Claude 3.5 to analyze student performance and provide feedback.

4. Implementation and Deployment:

Develop Custom Applications:

Build custom applications that integrate Claude 3.5 with industry-specific tools and systems.

Deploy Cloud-Based Solutions:

Leverage cloud platforms to deploy scalable and reliable AI workflows.

Integrate with Existing Systems:

Ensure seamless integration with existing industry-specific software and hardware.

Testing and Validation:

Thoroughly test and validate the AI workflow to ensure accuracy and reliability.

Continuous Monitoring and Improvement:

Monitor the performance of the AI workflow and make necessary adjustments based on user feedback and data analysis.

By creating custom AI workflows tailored to specific industries, businesses can unlock significant value and gain a competitive edge.

6.3 Optimizing Time Management and Decision-Making with AI Assistance"

Optimizing time management and decision-making with AI assistance, particularly using Claude 3.5, involves leveraging the model's capabilities to streamline tasks, analyze information, and provide insights that support efficient and effective decision-making.[1] Here's how:

1. Time Management Optimization:

Task Prioritization and Scheduling:

Use Claude 3.5 to analyze your to-do list, identify urgent and important tasks, and generate a prioritized schedule.

Example: "Analyze my to-do list and create a schedule for today, prioritizing tasks based on urgency and importance."

Automate the generation of reminders and alerts for upcoming deadlines or appointments.

Email and Communication Management:

Use Claude 3.5 to summarize lengthy emails, extract key information, and draft responses.[2]

Automate the sorting and filtering of emails based on content and sender.[3]

Generate summaries of communication threads.

Meeting Management:

Use Claude 3.5 to generate meeting agendas, take notes, and summarize key decisions.[4]

Automate the scheduling of meetings based on participants' availability.

Generate action items, based on meeting notes.[5]

Information Filtering:

Claude 3.5 can filter news articles, social media feeds, and other sources of information, only providing the user with relevant data.

2. Decision-Making Enhancement:

Data Analysis and Insight Generation:

Use Claude 3.5 to analyze data, identify trends, and generate insights that support informed decision-making.[6]

Example: "Analyze this sales data and identify the key factors contributing to the recent decline in revenue."

Generate summaries of complex reports or research papers.[7]

Scenario Planning and Risk Assessment:

Use Claude 3.5 to generate potential scenarios and assess the risks and benefits associated with each option.

Example: "Generate three possible scenarios for launching a new product and assess the potential risks and benefits of each scenario."

Generate possible outcomes based on different variables.

Information Retrieval and Knowledge Synthesis:

Use Claude 3.5 to retrieve relevant information from databases, knowledge bases, or the web.[8]

Synthesize information from multiple sources to provide a comprehensive overview of a topic.

Decision Support Systems:

Integrate Claude 3.5 with decision support systems to provide real-time insights and recommendations.

Automate the generation of reports and visualizations that support decision-making.[9]

Generating Pros and Cons Lists:

Claude 3.5 can generate lists of pros and cons, based on provided information.

3. Implementation Strategies:

API Integration:

Use Claude 3.5's API to integrate with existing productivity tools, such as calendars, email clients, and project management software.[10]

Custom Applications:

Develop custom applications that leverage Claude 3.5's capabilities to automate specific tasks and provide decision support.[11]

Natural Language Interfaces:

Create natural language interfaces that allow users to interact with Claude 3.5 using voice commands or text-based prompts.

Workflow Automation:

Design automated workflows that incorporate Claude 3.5 to streamline repetitive tasks and provide timely insights.[12]

Prompt Engineering:

Crafting very specific prompts, is very important.

4. Key Considerations:

Data Accuracy and Reliability:

Ensure that the data used by Claude 3.5 is accurate and reliable.

Privacy and Security:

Protect sensitive data and comply with relevant privacy regulations.

Human Oversight:

Use Claude 3.5 as a tool to augment human decision-making, not replace it.

Continuous Improvement:

Monitor the performance of Claude 3.5 and make necessary adjustments to optimize its effectiveness.

By effectively leveraging AI assistance, you can significantly enhance your time management and decision-making capabilities, leading to increased productivity and better outcomes.

Chapter 7

Claude 3.5 for Advanced Research and Analysis

7.1 Conducting Literature Reviews and Research Summaries"

1. Literature Review Strategies:

Keyword and Concept Identification:

Use Claude 3.5 to brainstorm relevant keywords and concepts related to your research topic.

Example: "Generate a list of keywords related to the impact of social media on mental health."

Source Identification and Retrieval:

Ask Claude 3.5 to suggest relevant research papers, articles, and books based on your keywords and research question.

While Claude 3.5 can't directly access paywalled content, it can suggest titles, authors, and databases.

Example: "Suggest relevant research papers on the topic of artificial intelligence in education."

Summarization and Synthesis:

Provide Claude 3.5 with abstracts or full texts of research papers and ask it to summarize the key findings, methodologies, and conclusions.

Example: "Summarize the key findings of this research paper on climate change."

Use Claude 3.5 to synthesize information from multiple sources and identify common themes, contradictions, or gaps in the literature.

Identifying Research Gaps:

Ask Claude 3.5 to identify research gaps, and suggest areas of further study.

Example: "Based on these research papers, what are some potential gaps in the current research?"

Creating annotated bibliographies:

Claude 3.5 can be used to create annotated bibliographies.

Example: "Summarize this article, and explain how it relates to my research."

2. Research Summary Techniques:

Abstract Generation:

Use Claude 3.5 to generate concise abstracts or summaries of research papers or reports.

Example: "Generate a 150-word abstract for this research paper on renewable energy."

Key Finding Extraction:

Instruct Claude 3.5 to extract the most important findings, conclusions, and implications from a research paper.

Example: "Extract the key findings and conclusions from this study on the effects of exercise on cognitive function."

Methodology Summarization:

Ask Claude 3.5 to summarize the research methodology, including the study design, data collection methods, and statistical analysis.

Example: "Summarize the research methodology used in this study on consumer behavior."

Comparison and Contrast:

Use Claude 3.5 to compare studies on the effectiveness of online learning."

Generating Report Outlines:

Claude 3.5 can be used to generate report outlines, based on the research.

Example: "Generate an outline for a research report on the effects of air pollution on children's health."

3. Best Practices:

Provide Clear Instructions:

Use specific and detailed prompts to guide Claude 3.5's responses.

Use Contextual Information:

Provide Claude 3.5 with relevant background information and context to improve the accuracy of its summaries and analyses.

Iterative Refinement:

Review and refine Claude 3.5's outputs to ensure accuracy and completeness.

Fact-Checking:

Always verify the information provided by Claude 3.5 with original sources, especially for critical research.

Citation Management:

Use citation management tools to organize and format your references.

Use Delimiters:

Using things like triple quotes, or triple dashes, can help the AI understand where sections of the prompt begin, and end.

Few shot learning:

Providing a few examples can greatly help the AI understand the desired output.

By effectively utilizing Claude 3.5, researchers can significantly enhance their literature review and research summary processes, leading to more efficient and insightful research outcomes.

7.2 Analyzing Complex Documents and Scientific Papers"

Analyzing complex documents and scientific papers with Claude 3.5 requires a strategic approach to leverage its natural language processing capabilities effectively. Here's a detailed guide:

1. Preprocessing and Understanding the Document:

Document Loading and Formatting:

If possible, convert documents to a text-based format (e.g., .txt, .pdf with text extraction) for optimal processing.

Understand the document's structure, including sections, headings, figures, and tables.

Key Concept Identification:

Use Claude 3.5 to identify key concepts, terms, and acronyms within the document.

Example: "Identify the main concepts and acronyms used in this scientific paper."

Contextual Understanding:

Provide Claude 3.5 with context about the document's purpose, scope, and target audienceThis helps the model understand the nuances of the language used.

2. Information Extraction and Analysis:

Summarization and Abstracting:

Use Claude 3.5 to generate summaries of specific sections or the entire document.[1]

Example: "Summarize the methodology section of this research paper."

Ask for abstractive summaries to capture the essence of the content.

Data Extraction from Tables and Figures:

If the document contains tables or figures, ask Claude 3.5 to describe the data and extract key values.

Example: "Describe the data presented in Figure 2 and extract the key findings."

Claude 3.5 Sonnet, having vision capabilities, will be especially useful here.

Identifying Key Arguments and Evidence:

Instruct Claude 3.5 to identify the main arguments, hypotheses, and supporting evidence presented in the document.

Example: "Identify the main arguments and supporting evidence presented in this policy document."

Comparison and Contrast:

If analyzing multiple documents, use Claude 3.5 to compare and contrast their findings, methodologies, and conclusions.[2]

Example: "Compare and contrast the methodologies used in these two scientific papers."

Identifying Biases and Limitations:

Ask Claude 3.5 to find possible biases within the document, or possible limitations to the research.

Example: "What are some possible limitations to this study?"

3. Generating Insights and Reports:

Synthesis of Information:

Use Claude 3.5 to synthesize information from various sections of the document and generate a cohesive report.

Example: "Synthesize the findings from the results and discussion sections of this scientific paper."

Answering Specific Questions:

Ask Claude 3.5 specific questions about the document to extract relevant information.

Example: "What were the main conclusions of this study regarding the effects of X on Y?"

Generating Actionable Insights:

Instruct Claude 3.5 to generate actionable insights or recommendations based on the document's content.

Example: "Based on the findings of this report, what are the recommended actions for policymakers?"

Creating Report Outlines:

Claude 3.5 can be used to generate report outlines based on the analysis of complex documents.

Example: "Generate an outline for a report summarizing the key findings of this white paper."

4. Best Practices:

Break Down Complex Tasks:

Divide complex documents into smaller sections and analyze them individually.

Use Clear and Specific Prompts:

Provide detailed instructions to guide Claude 3.5's analysis.

Iterative Refinement:

Refine your prompts based on the model's responses to improve accuracy.

Verify Information:

Always verify the information provided by Claude 3.5 with the original document.

Use Delimiters:

Using things like triple quotes, or triple dashes, can help the AI understand where sections of the prompt begin, and end.

Few shot learning:

Providing examples of the desired output can greatly help the AI understand the request.

Combine with Human Expertise:

Use Claude 3.5 as a tool to augment human analysis, not replace it.

By following these strategies, you can effectively leverage Claude 3.5 to analyze complex documents and scientific papers, extracting valuable insights and generating comprehensive reports.

7.3 Using AI to Identify Trends and Emerging Patterns"

Using AI, specifically Claude 3.5, to identify trends and emerging patterns involves leveraging its ability to process and analyze large volumes of data, both structured and unstructured, to uncover hidden insights. Here's how to approach this:

1. Data Collection and Preparation:

Gather Relevant Data:

Identify the data sources relevant to your trend analysis. This could include social media data, news articles, market research reports, scientific publications, or internal business data.

Claude 3.5 can process text data, and Claude 3.5 Sonnet can also process images.

Data Cleaning and Preprocessing:

Clean and preprocess the data to remove noise, inconsistencies, and irrelevant information.

Format the data into a structure that Claude 3.5 can easily process (e.g., text files, CSV, JSON).

2. Trend Identification and Analysis:

Topic Modeling and Keyword Extraction:

Use Claude 3.5 to identify key topics and keywords within the data.

This helps uncover emerging themes and areas of interest.

Example: "Identify the main topics and keywords discussed in these social media posts."

Sentiment Analysis:

Analyze the sentiment expressed in the data to understand public opinion and attitudes towards specific topics.

This can help identify shifts in public perception and emerging trends.

Example: "Analyze the sentiment expressed in these customer reviews and identify any emerging trends."

Pattern Recognition:

Instruct Claude 3.5 to identify recurring patterns and correlations within the data.

This can help uncover hidden relationships and emerging trends.

Example: "Identify any recurring patterns in these sales data and explain their potential significance."

Time Series Analysis:

If the data includes timestamps, use Claude 3.5 to analyze trends over time.

This can help identify seasonal patterns, growth trends, and other temporal variations.

Example: "Analyze these website traffic data and identify any seasonal trends."

Anomaly Detection:

Ask Claude 3.5 to identify any unusual or unexpected data points.

These anomalies can indicate emerging trends or significant shifts in the data.

3. Generating Insights and Predictions:

Trend Summarization:

Use Claude 3.5 to summarize the identified trends and explain their potential implications.

Example: "Summarize the key trends identified in these market research reports and explain their potential impact on the industry."

Emerging Pattern Prediction:

Based on the identified trends and patterns, ask Claude 3.5 to generate predictions about future developments.

Example: "Based on the identified trends in social media data, predict the future direction of this consumer trend."

Generating Reports:

Claude 3.5 can generate reports that describe the discovered trends.

Example: "Generate a report describing the emerging trends in AI development."

Generating visual descriptions:

If you have charts or graphs that show trends, you can ask Claude 3.5 to describe those visualizations.

4. Best Practices:

Data Quality:

Ensure that the data used for trend analysis is accurate and reliable.

Clear Prompts:

Use clear and specific prompts to guide Claude 3.5's analysis.

Iterative Analysis:

Refine your analysis based on the model's responses and insights.

Human Validation:

Always validate the identified trends and predictions with human expertise.

Contextual Awareness:

Provide Claude 3.5 with as much context as possible.

Few shot learning:

Providing examples of the desired output can greatly enhance the AI's performance.

By following these strategies, you can effectively use Claude 3.5 to identify trends and emerging patterns, gaining valuable insights that can inform strategic decision-making.

Chapter 8

Customizing and Fine-Tuning Claude 3.5 Models

8.1 Understanding Model Parameters and Configuration Options"

Understanding the model parameters and configuration options of Claude 3.5 is crucial for fine-tuning its performance and tailoring it to specific tasks. Here's a breakdown of the key aspects:

1. Core Parameters and Their Functions:

Model Selection:

Claude 3.5 offers different model variations (e.g., Sonnet, Haiku), each with varying levels of capability and performance.

Understanding the differences between these models is essential for selecting the appropriate one for your needs.

Temperature:

This parameter controls the randomness of the model's output.

A higher temperature (e.g., 0.8) results in more creative and unpredictable responses, while a lower temperature (e.g., 0.2) produces more deterministic and focused outputs.

Explain how this influences the diversity of generated text.

Max Tokens to Sample:

This parameter limits the length of the model's output.

Understanding how to set this parameter appropriately is crucial for controlling the length of responses and avoiding excessive output.

Top-K and Top-P (Nucleus Sampling):

These parameters control the selection of tokens during the generation process.

Top-K limits the selection to the top K most likely tokens, while Top-P (nucleus sampling) limits the selection to a dynamic set of tokens whose cumulative probability exceeds a certain threshold.

Explain how these parameters influence the diversity and coherence of the output.

Stop Sequences:

These parameters define sequences of tokens that will cause the model to stop generating output.

This is useful for controlling the length and format of responses.

2. Configuration Options and Their Impact:

Prompt Engineering Techniques:

While not strictly "parameters," the way you structure your prompts significantly impacts the model's behavior.

Explain the importance of clear and specific prompts, few-shot learning, and role-playing.

Context Window Management:

Understanding the size of Claude 3.5's context window is crucial for managing long conversations and documents.

Explain how to effectively utilize the context window to maintain coherence and relevance.

Safety and Alignment Settings:

Anthropic emphasizes safety and alignment, so understanding how these settings influence the model's behavior is essential.

Explain how the "Constitutional AI" influences the models responses.

API Usage and Rate Limits:

Understanding API rate limits and usage quotas is essential for preventing interruptions and optimizing performance.

Explain how to handle API errors.

Data Input Formats:

Explain the best data input formats for the AI. For example, how to use delimiters.

3. Fine-Tuning Considerations:

Task-Specific Optimization:

Explain how to adjust parameters and configuration options to optimize performance for specific tasks, such as summarization, question answering, or code generation.

Experimentation and Evaluation:

Emphasize the importance of experimentation and evaluation to determine the optimal parameter settings for your specific use case.

Explain how to measure and evaluate the model's performance.

Iterative Refinement:

Explain how to iteratively refine your prompts and parameter settings based on the model's outputs.

Understanding the trade offs:

Explain the trade offs between speed, accuracy, and randomness.

4. Documentation and Resources:

Anthropic API Documentation:

Emphasize the importance of consulting the official Anthropic API documentation for the most up-to-date information on model parameters and configuration options.

Community Forums and Resources:

Encourage readers to explore community forums and resources for tips and best practices.

By understanding these model parameters and configuration options, users can effectively fine-tune Claude 3.5 to achieve optimal performance for their specific needs.

8.2 Fine-Tuning Claude 3.5 for Specific Domains and Tasks"

Fine-tuning Claude 3.5 for specific domains and tasks allows you to significantly enhance its performance and tailor it to your precise needs. While direct fine-tuning of the core model might not be publicly available in the traditional sense, you can achieve similar results through effective prompt engineering and by leveraging the model's adaptability. Here's a comprehensive guide:

1. Domain-Specific Adaptation Through Prompt Engineering:

Few-Shot Learning:

Provide Claude 3.5 with several examples of the desired output for your specific domain or task.

This helps the model learn the patterns, style, and terminology relevant to your area of expertise.

Example: If you're working in the legal domain, provide examples of legal briefs or contracts.

Role-Playing and Persona Assignment:

Instruct Claude 3.5 to adopt a specific persona or role relevant to your domain.

This helps the model generate responses that are consistent with the expertise and perspective of that persona.

Example: "You are a seasoned medical researcher. Analyze this patient's medical history and provide a diagnosis."

Domain-Specific Terminology and Jargon:

Use the specific terminology and jargon relevant to your domain in your prompts.

This helps Claude 3.5 understand the context and generate more accurate responses.

Contextual Priming:

Provide the model with contextual information before giving it the main prompt.

This will allow the AI to have the correct background information needed to provide the best possible output.

2. Task-Specific Optimization:

Summarization:

Provide clear instructions regarding the desired length, level of detail, and focus of the summary.

Use specific keywords or phrases to guide the model's attention.

Question Answering:

Provide the model with relevant context or background information before asking the question.

Use clear and specific questions to elicit the desired information.

Code Generation:

Provide detailed instructions regarding the desired functionality, input parameters, and output values.

Use code examples or templates to guide the model's output.

Data Analysis:

Provide the AI with clear instructions about what data to analyze, and what you are looking for.

Example: "Analyze this CSV file, and give me the average of the third column."

Creative writing:

Provide the AI with the desired tone, style, and length of the desired creative work.

Example: "Write a poem that is 14 lines long, that is in the style of Edgar Allen Poe."

3. Data Augmentation and Knowledge Bases:

External Knowledge Integration:

Provide Claude 3.5 with access to relevant external knowledge bases or databases.

This can be achieved by providing the model with relevant information in the prompt or by integrating with external APIs.

Data Augmentation:

Augment your prompts with relevant data or examples to improve the model's performance.

This can be particularly useful for tasks that require specific knowledge or expertise.

4. Iterative Refinement and Evaluation:

Experimentation and Evaluation:

Experiment with different prompts and techniques to determine the optimal approach for your specific domain or task.

Evaluate the model's performance based on relevant metrics and user feedback.

Iterative Refinement:

Continuously refine your prompts and techniques based on the model's outputs and evaluation results.

This iterative process helps you achieve optimal performance over time.

5. Key Considerations:

Prompt Clarity:

Clear and specific prompts are essential for effective fine-tuning.

Data Quality:

The quality of the data used for few-shot learning and knowledge integration significantly impacts performance.

Ethical Considerations:

Be mindful of potential biases or harmful content in the model's outputs.

API Limitations:

Be aware of API rate limits, and context window limitations.

By following these strategies, you can effectively fine-tune Claude 3.5 for specific domains and tasks, significantly enhancing its performance and tailoring it to your precise needs.

8.3 Implementing Custom Training Data for Enhanced Performance"

Implementing custom training data for enhanced performance with Claude 3.5, while not involving traditional model retraining in the public API sense, can be achieved through techniques that effectively simulate fine-tuning. Here's a detailed guide:

1. Understanding the Concept of "Custom Training Data" in this Context:

Prompt Engineering as "Training":

Since direct model retraining is typically not available via the API, "custom training data" refers to the examples and context you provide within your prompts.

This data shapes the model's responses and guides its behavior for specific tasks.

Focus on Few-Shot Learning:

Few-shot learning is the primary method for leveraging custom data. You provide a few examples of the desired input-output pairs to demonstrate the task.

This helps Claude 3.5 understand the patterns and relationships specific to your domain.

2. Gathering and Preparing Custom Training Data:

Identify Relevant Data:

Gather data that is representative of the tasks and domains you want to optimize.

This could include:

Domain-specific documents or articles.

Examples of desired output formats (e.g., summaries, reports, code snippets).

Question-answer pairs relevant to your use case.

Data Cleaning and Formatting:

Ensure that your data is clean, consistent, and free of errors.

Format the data into a structure that Claude 3.5 can easily process.

Use delimiters (e.g., triple quotes, triple dashes) to clearly separate input and output examples.

Data Augmentation:

Create variations of your data to increase the diversity of your training examples.

This can help the model generalize better to unseen data.

3. Implementing Custom Data in Prompts:

Few-Shot Learning Examples:

Include several examples of input-output pairs in your prompts.

Clearly label the input and output sections of each example.

Example:

Input: "Translate 'hello' to French."
Output: "Bonjour"

Input: "Translate 'goodbye' to French."
Output: "Au revoir"

Input: "Translate 'thank you' to French."
Output:

Contextual Priming:

Provide relevant context or background information before presenting the examples.

This helps the model understand the domain andtask.

Domain-Specific Terminology:

Use the specific terminology and jargon relevant to your domain in your examples.

This helps the model learn the language patterns specific to your area of expertise.

4. Iterative Refinement and Evaluation:

Experimentation:

Experiment with different sets of examples and prompt structures to find the most effective approach.

Vary the number and diversity of your examples.

Evaluation:

Evaluate the model's performance based on relevant metrics and user feedback.

Identify areas for improvement and adjust your prompts accordingly.

Iterative Improvement:

Continuously refine your custom data and prompt engineering techniques based on the model's outputs and evaluation results.

Keep records of what prompts provide the best output.

5. Key Considerations:

Data Relevance:

Ensure that your custom data is highly relevant to your specific tasks and domains.

Data Quality:

The quality of your custom data significantly impacts the model's performance.

Prompt Clarity:

Clear and concise prompts are essential for effective few-shot learning.

API Limitations:

Be aware of API rate limits and context window limitations.

Ethical Considerations:

Be aware of any biases within your data, and how that can effect the AI's output.

By implementing custom training data through effective prompt engineering and few-shot learning, you can significantly enhance Claude 3.5's performance and tailor it to your specific needs.

Chapter 9

Ethical Considerations and Responsible AI Use

9.1 Addressing Bias and Fairness in AI-Generated Content"

Addressing bias and fairness in AI-generated content is a critical aspect of responsible AI development and deployment. Here's a comprehensive guide on how to approach this challenge with Claude 3.5:

1. Understanding the Sources of Bias:

Data Bias:

Recognize that AI models learn from the data they are trained on, which may contain biases reflecting societal inequalities.

This can lead to AI-generated content that perpetuates or amplifies existing biases.

Algorithmic Bias:

Be aware that the algorithms used to train AI models can also introduce biases, even if the training data is seemingly unbiased.

This can occur due to the way the model learns and generalizes from the data.

Human Bias:

Acknowledge that human biases can influence the design, development, and deployment of AI systems.

This can manifest in the choice of training data, the definition of fairness metrics, and the interpretation of results.

2. Strategies for Mitigating Bias:

Data Auditing and Preprocessing:

Carefully audit your training data for potential biases.

Use techniques such as data augmentation, re-sampling, or re-weighting to address imbalances in the data.

Fairness-Aware Training:

Employ fairness-aware training techniques, such as adversarial training or regularization, to mitigate bias in the model's outputs.

This may involve defining and optimizing for specific fairness metrics.

Prompt Engineering for Fairness:

Craft prompts that explicitly instruct Claude 3.5 to avoid biased or discriminatory language.

Use role-playing or persona assignment to encourage the model to consider diverse perspectives.

Contextual Awareness:

Provide Claude 3.5 with context about the target audience and the intended purpose of the content.

This helps the model generate responses that are appropriate and sensitive to the specific context.

Red Teaming and Adversarial Testing:

Conduct red teaming exercises to identify potential biases in the model's outputs.

Use adversarial testing to evaluate the model's robustness to biased inputs.

Monitoring and Evaluation:

Continuously monitor the model's outputs for potential biases.

Use fairness metrics to evaluate the model's performance and identify areas for improvement.

Feedback Loops:

Implement feedback loops to gather user input on potential biases in the model's outputs.

Use this feedback to refine the model and improve its fairness.

Transparency:

Be transparent about the limitations of AI models and the potential for bias in their outputs.

Clearly communicate the steps taken to mitigate bias.

3. Specific Techniques for Claude 3.5:

Constitutional AI:

Leverage Anthropic's "Constitutional AI" approach, which guides the model's behavior based on a set of ethical principles.

This helps ensure that the model generates responses that are helpful, harmless, and honest.

Few-Shot Learning with Diverse Examples:

Use few-shot learning with examples that represent diverse perspectives and avoid reinforcing stereotypes.

This helps the model learn to generate responses that are inclusive and equitable.

Prompting for Counterfactuals:

Ask Claude 3.5 to generate counterfactual examples to identify potential biases in its reasoning.

Example: "If the person in this scenario were of a different race, would the outcome be the same?"

Using Delimiters:

Using things like triple quotes, or triple dashes, can help the AI understand where sections of the prompt begin, and end. This is useful when providing context, and examples.

4. Ethical Considerations:

Define Fairness Metrics:

Clearly define what fairness means in the context of your specific application.

Use appropriate fairness metrics to evaluate the model's performance.

Consider Intersectionality:

Recognize that individuals can belong to multiple marginalized groups, and that biases can intersect in complex ways.

Consider intersectional fairness metrics to address these complexities.

Engage with Stakeholders:

Engage with diverse stakeholders, including marginalized communities, to understand their perspectives and concerns.

Incorporate their feedback into the development and deployment of AI systems.

By implementing these strategies, you can effectively address bias and fairness in AI-generated content, ensuring that Claude 3.5 is used responsibly and ethically.

9.2 Ensuring Data Privacy and Security in AI Applications"

Ensuring data privacy and security in AI applications, particularly those leveraging models like Claude 3.5, is paramount. Here's a comprehensive guide to address these critical aspects:

1. Data Minimization and Purpose Limitation:

Collect Only Necessary Data:

Adhere to the principle of data minimization by collecting only the data that is strictly necessary for the AI application's intended purpose.[1]

Avoid collecting sensitive data that is not essential.[2]

Define Clear Purposes:

Clearly define the purposes for which data is collected and used.[3]

Ensure that data is not used for purposes that are incompatible with the original purpose of collection.[4]

2. Data Encryption and Secure Storage:

Encrypt Data at Rest and in Transit:

Encrypt sensitive data both when it is stored (at rest) and when it is transmitted (in transit).[5]

Use strong encryption algorithms and protocols.[6]

Secure Storage Practices:

Store data in secure environments with access controls and audit trails.

Implement robust security measures to prevent unauthorized access, use, or disclosure of data.

Anonymization and Pseudonymization:

When possible, anonymize or pseudonymize data to reduce the risk of re-identification.[8]

Anonymization removes all personally identifiable information (PII), while pseudonymization replaces PII with pseudonyms.[9]

3. Access Control and Authorization:

Principle of Least Privilege:

Implement the principle of least privilege by granting users only the minimum level of access necessary to perform their tasks.

Use role-based access control (RBAC) to manage user permissions.[10]

Strong Authentication and Authorization:

Use strong authentication methods, such as multi-factor authentication (MFA), to verify user identities.[11]

Implement robust authorization mechanisms to control access to data and resources.[12]

4. API Security and Data Transmission:

Secure API Endpoints:

Secure API endpoints with authentication and authorization mechanisms.[13]

Use HTTPS to encrypt data transmitted over the network.[14]

Input Validation and Sanitization:

Validate and sanitize user inputs to prevent injection attacks and other security vulnerabilities.[15]

Carefully handle user-provided data that is used in prompts.[16]

Rate Limiting and Throttling:

Implement rate limiting and throttling to prevent abuse and denial-of-service attacks.

5. Compliance with Data Privacy Regulations:

GDPR, CCPA, and Other Regulations:

Ensure compliance with relevant data privacy regulations, such as GDPR, CCPA, and HIPAA.

Understand the specific requirements of these regulations and implement appropriate safeguards.

Data Subject Rights:

Respect data subject rights, such as the right to access, rectify, and erase personal data.[17]

Implement mechanisms to handle data subject requests.[18]

6. Model Security and Vulnerability Management:

Model Auditing and Testing:

Regularly audit and test AI models for potential security vulnerabilities.[19]

Conduct penetration testing and vulnerability assessments.[20]

Model Updates and Patching:

Keep AI models and related software up to date with the latest security patches.[21]

Address security vulnerabilities promptly.[22]

Secure Model Deployment:

Deploy AI models in secure environments with access controls and monitoring.[23]

7. Transparency and Accountability:

Data Usage Policies:

Develop clear and transparent data usage policies that explain how data is collected, used, and protected.[24]

Communicate these policies to users in a clear and understandable manner.[25]

Audit Trails and Logging:

Implement audit trails and logging to track data access and usage.[26]

This helps identify and investigate security incidents.

Responsible AI Practices:

Adhere to responsible AI practices, including fairness, accountability, and transparency.[27]

Ensure that AI applications are developed and deployed ethically.

8. User Education and Awareness:

Privacy Training:

Provide users with training on data privacy and security best practices.

Educate users about the risks of phishing, social engineering, and other security threats.

Data Handling Guidelines:

Develop and communicate clear data handling guidelines for users.[28]

Emphasize the importance of protecting sensitive data.

By implementing these measures, you can significantly enhance data privacy and security in AI applications, ensuring that user data is protected and that AI systems are used responsibly.

9.3 Implementing Ethical Guidelines for AI Development and Deploymen

Implementing ethical guidelines for AI development and deployment is crucial for ensuring that AI systems are used responsibly and beneficially. Here's a comprehensive guide:

1. Establishing Ethical Principles:

Define Core Values:

Identify the fundamental ethical principles that will guide your AI development and deployment.

These principles may include fairness, transparency, accountability, privacy, and safety.

Stakeholder Engagement:

Engage with diverse stakeholders, includingethicists, domain experts, and affected communities, to develop ethical guidelines.

Incorporate their perspectives and concerns into the guidelines.

Alignment with Existing Frameworks:

Align your ethical guidelines with established frameworks and standards, such as those developed by the OECD, UNESCO, or the EU.

2. Developing Ethical Guidelines:

Fairness and Non-Discrimination:

Ensure that AI systems are designed and deployed in a way that avoids bias and discrimination.

Implement fairness metrics and conduct regular audits to assess and mitigate bias.

Transparency and Explainability:

Strive for transparency in AI systems by making their decision-making processes understandable.

Implement explainability techniques to provideinsights into how AI models arrive at their conclusions.

Accountability and Responsibility:

Establish clear lines of accountability for the development and deployment of AI systems.

Design mechanisms for human oversight and intervention.

Privacy and Data Protection:

Protect user privacy by adhering to data privacy regulations and implementing robust security measures.

Minimize data collection and ensure that data is used only for its intended purpose.

Safety and Security:

Prioritize the safety and security of AI systems by conducting thorough testing and risk assessments.

Implement safeguards to prevent misuse or unintended harm.

Human Oversight and Control:

Maintain human oversight and control over AI systems, particularly in critical applications.

Ensure that humans can intervene or override AI decisions when necessary.

Social Impact and Well-Being:

Consider the broader social impact of AI systems and strive to promote well-being.

Address potential negative consequences, such as job displacement or the spread of misinformation.

3. Implementing Ethical Guidelines:

Integrate Ethics into Development Processes:

Incorporate ethical considerations into all stages of the AI development lifecycle, from design to deployment.

Use ethical impact assessments to identify and mitigate potential risks.

Establish Ethical Review Boards:

Create ethical review boards to oversee AI projects and ensure compliance with ethical guidelines.

Include diverse perspectives and expertise on these boards.

Develop Training and Education Programs:

Provide training and education programs for AI developers and stakeholders on ethical principles and best practices.

Raise awareness about the potential ethical implications of AI.

Implement Monitoring and Auditing Mechanisms:

Establish mechanisms to monitor and audit AI systems for compliance with ethical guidelines.

Conduct regular reviews and assessments to identify areas for improvement.

Establish Whistleblowing Channels:

Create safe and confidential channels for reporting ethical concerns or violations.

Document Everything:

Keep detailed records of the process of ethical consideration, and implementation.

4. Continuous Improvement:

Regularly Review and Update Guidelines:

Regularly review and update ethical guidelines to reflect evolving best practices and societal values.

Adapt to new technologies and emerging ethical challenges.

Foster a Culture of Ethics:

Cultivate a culture of ethics within your organization by promoting open dialogue and critical thinking.

Encourage employees to raise ethical concerns and provide feedback.

Collaborate and Share Best Practices:

Collaborate with other organizations and stakeholders to share best practices and lessons learned.

Contribute to the development of industry-wide ethical standards.

By implementing these guidelines, organizations can ensure that AI systems are developed and deployed responsibly, ethically, and for the benefit of society.

Chapter 10

The Future of Claude 3.5 and AI Communication

10.1 Exploring Emerging Trends in AI and Natural Language Processing"

Exploring emerging trends in AI and Natural Language Processing (NLP) is crucial for staying ahead in this rapidly evolving field.[1] Here's a look at some of the key trends shaping the future:

1. Multimodal AI:

Integration of Multiple Modalities:

AI systems are increasingly integrating multiple modalities, such as text, images, audio, and video.[2]

This allows for more comprehensive understanding and generation of information.[3]

Vision-Language Models:

Models that can understand and reason about both visual and textual data are becoming more sophisticated.[4]

Applications include image captioning, visual question answering, and multimodal search.[5]

Audio and Speech Processing:

Advances in speech recognition, synthesis, and understanding are enabling more natural and intuitive human-computer interactions.[6]

2. Large Language Models (LLMs) Advancements:

Increased Context Windows:

LLMs are expanding their context windows, allowing them to process and understand longer sequences of text.[7]

This improves their ability to handle complex tasks, such as document summarization and long-form conversation.[8]

Improved Reasoning and Problem-Solving:

LLMs are demonstrating enhanced reasoning and problem-solving abilities, enabling them to tackle more complex tasks.[9]

This includes improvements in logical reasoning, mathematical reasoning, and common-sense reasoning.[10]

Efficiency and Optimization:

Researchers are focusing on optimizing LLMs for efficiency, reducing their computational cost and energy consumption.[11]

This includes techniques such as model distillation, quantization, and pruning.[12]

Specialized LLMs:

The creation of LLMs that are focused on very specific tasks, or fields.[13] This allows for increased accuracy within those fields.

3. Ethical AI and Responsible Development:

Bias Mitigation and Fairness:

Increased focus on mitigating bias and ensuring fairness in AI systems.[14]

Development of techniques for detecting and mitigating bias in training data and model outputs.[15]

Transparency and Explainability:

Efforts to make AI systems more transparent and explainable, enabling users to understand how they arrive at their decisions.[16]

This includes techniques such as explainable AI (XAI).[17]

Privacy and Security:

Emphasis on protecting user privacy and ensuring the security of AI systems.[18]

Development of techniques for privacy-preserving machine learning and secure model deployment.[19]

AI Safety:

A large increase in the focus of AI safety, and making sure that AI systems are aligned with human values.[20]

4. NLP for Specific Applications:

Healthcare:

NLP is being used to analyze medical records, extract insights from clinical notes, and develop AI-powered diagnostic tools.[21]

Finance:

NLP is being used to analyze financial news, detect fraud, and generate personalized financial reports.[22]

Legal:

NLP is being used to analyze legal documents, extract relevant information, and automate legal research.[23]

Education:

NLP is being used to create personalized learning experiences, and to automate grading.[24]

Customer Service:

LLMs are being used to create very advanced chatbots, that can handle complex customer support requests.[25]

5. Advancements in NLP Techniques:

Reinforcement Learning from Human Feedback (RLHF):

This technique is used to align LLMs with human preferences and values.

It involves training models to generate responses that are rated highly by human evaluators.

Knowledge Graphs and Semantic Understanding:

Knowledge graphs are being used to enhance the semantic understanding of NLP systems.[26]

This allows AI models to reason about relationships between entities and concepts.

Low-Resource NLP:

Researchers are developing techniques for building NLP systems that can operate effectively with limited training data.

This is particularly important for languages and domains with scarce resources.

Edge AI NLP:

Running NLP models on edge devices, instead of in the cloud.[27] This allows for faster processing, and increased privacy.

By staying informed about these emerging trends, you can effectively leverage the latest advancements in AI and NLP to create innovative and impactful applications.

10.2 Predicting the Evolution of Claude 3.5 and its Capabilities"

Predicting the precise evolution of any AI model is inherently challenging, given the rapid pace of innovation in the field. However, by analyzing Anthropic's trajectory and the broader trends in AI, we can make some informed predictions about the future of Claude 3.5 and its capabilities.

Here are some key areas where we can anticipate future developments:

1. Enhanced Multimodal Capabilities:

Given the advancements in multimodal AI, it's highly likely that Claude 3.5 will see further enhancements in its ability to process and integrate information from various modalities.

This could involve improved understanding of video, audio, and other sensory data, leading to more sophisticated applications.

Especially with the current capabilities of Claude 3.5 Sonnet, expect improvements in image understanding, and the combination of image and text analysis.

2. Increased Efficiency and Scalability:

Anthropic, like other AI developers, will continue to focus on optimizing the efficiency and scalability of its models.

This could involve advancements in model architecture, training techniques, and hardware acceleration.

Expect to see Claude 3.5 become faster, more resource-efficient, and capable of handling larger workloads.

3. Deeper Contextual Understanding and Reasoning:

A key area of development will be to further enhance Claude 3.5's ability to understand and reason about complex contexts.

This could involve improvements in its ability to handle long-range dependencies, understand nuanced language, and perform more sophisticated reasoning tasks.

Increasing the context window size, will likely continue to be a focus.

4. Stronger Focus on Ethical AI and Safety:

Anthropic's commitment to AI safety and responsible development will continue to be a driving force in the evolution of Claude 3.5.

Expect to see further advancements in techniques for mitigating bias, ensuring fairness, and enhancing the transparency and explainability of AI systems.

Constitutional AI will likely be further developed.

5. Greater Customization and Specialization:

As AI becomes more integrated into various industries, there will be a growing demand for customized and specialized models.

Anthropic may develop tools and techniques that allow users to more easily fine-tune Claude 3.5 for specific domains and tasks.

This could involve the creation of domain-specific models or the development of more flexible prompt engineering techniques.

6. Enhanced Integration and Interoperability:

Claude 3.5 will likely see increased integration with other software applications and platforms.

This will enable seamless workflows and allow users to leverage the model's capabilities in a wider range of contexts.

Expect improvements in API functionality, and ease of use.

In essence, the future of Claude 3.5 will likely be characterized by:

Increased capabilities.

Greater efficiency.

A continued emphasis on ethical considerations.

By staying informed about these trends, users can prepare to effectively leverage the evolving capabilities of Claude 3.5.

10.3 Preparing for the Next Generation of AI-Driven Communication"

Preparing for the next generation of AI-driven communication requires a proactive and adaptable approach. Here's a comprehensive guide to help you navigate this evolving landscape:

1. Understanding the Changing Communication Landscape:

Rise of AI-Powered Tools:

Recognize the increasing prevalence of AI-powered communication tools, such as chatbots, virtual assistants, and automated content generation.

Understand how these tools are transforming communication patterns and expectations.

Shift Towards Natural Language Interfaces:

Anticipate a greater reliance on natural language interfaces for human-computer interaction.

Familiarize yourself with the capabilities and limitations of NLP technologies.

Personalized and Contextual Communication:

Prepare for communication experiences that are highly personalized and context-aware.

Understand how AI can leverage data to tailor messages and interactions to individual users.

Increased Multimodal Communication:

Recognize that communication will increasingly involve multiple modalities, such as text, voice, images, and video.

Develop skills in creating and interpreting multimodal content.

2. Developing Essential Skills and Competencies:

Prompt Engineering:

Master the art of crafting effective prompts for AI communication tools.

Learn how to provide clear instructions, specify desired outputs, and refine prompts based on AI responses.

Critical Evaluation of AI-Generated Content:

Develop the ability to critically evaluate AI-generated content for accuracy, bias, and ethical considerations.

Learn how to identify and mitigate potential risks associated with AI-generated information.

Human-AI Collaboration:

Embrace the concept of human-AI collaboration and learn how to work effectively with AI communication tools.

Understand how to leverage AI to augment human capabilities and enhance communication outcomes.

Ethical Communication Practices:

Develop a strong understanding of ethical communication principles and apply them to AI-driven interactions.

Promote transparency, accountability, and responsible use of AI communication tools.

Adaptability and Lifelong Learning:

Cultivate a mindset of adaptability and lifelong learning to keep pace with the rapid advancements in AI communication.

Stay informed about emerging trends and technologies.

3. Adapting Communication Strategies:

Embrace AI-Powered Tools:

Explore and adopt AI-powered communication tools that can enhance efficiency and effectiveness.

Integrate these tools into existing workflows and communication channels.

Develop AI Communication Policies:

Establish clear policies and guidelines for the use of AI communication tools within your organization.

Address issues such as data privacy, security, and ethical considerations.

Train Employees on AI Communication:

Provide training and education programs for employees on how to use AI communication tools effectively and responsibly.

Promote best practices and address potential challenges.

Focus on Human Connection:

While AI can enhance communication, it's essential to maintain a focus on human connection and empathy.

Use AI to augment, not replace, human interaction.

Monitor and Evaluate AI Communication:

Continuously monitor and evaluate the effectiveness of AI communication strategies.

Make adjustments based on data analysis and user feedback.

4. Addressing Ethical and Societal Implications:

Promote Responsible AI Development:

Support the development and deployment of AI communication tools that adhere to ethical principles and promote societal well-being.

Advocate for AI Literacy:

Raise awareness about the capabilities and limitations of AI communication technologies.

Promote AI literacy among the general public.

Engage in Dialogue and Collaboration:

Participate in discussions and collaborations with stakeholders to address the ethical and societal implications of AI communication.

Contribute to the development of industry standards and best practices.

Prepare for Misinformation:

AI will increase the ability to generate misinformation. Prepare for this by encouraging critical thinking.

By proactively preparing for the next generation of AI-driven communication, you can leverage its transformative potential while mitigating potential risks and ensuring ethical and responsible use.